"Solonche is productive and prolific, but that doesn't water down his poetry… He can compress a philosophical treatise into three lines… His epigrammatic tidy poems are philosophic gems. Solonche sees humor and encapsulates it; he frames a thought in perfect verse… He's playful and profound — the more he writes, the more he seems to know. Beneath the Solonche simplicity are significant social comments, and his goodwill reinforces the best in us."

— Grace Cavalieri, *Washington Independent Review of Books*

"Solonche, an accomplished poet, employs various forms in this compilation, including haiku, prose poem, and free verse. The poems often imaginatively enter into the natural or material world via anthropomorphic similes… Many works have an aphoristic quality that recall Zen koans, and they can be playfully amusing or even silly… A strong set of sympathetic but never sentimental observations."

— *Kirkus Reviews*

"The spirit of Horace, the melancholy of time slithering away and turning all to dust, tempered with art, wit, and good grace…"

— Ricardo Nirenberg, editor of *Offcourse: A Literary Journal*

"In a style that favors brevity and pith, J.R. Solonche brings a richness of experience, observation, and wit into his poems. Here is the world! they exclaim. And here, and here, and here! Watched over by ancient lyric gods – Time, Death, and Desire — we find the quotidian here transformed."

— Christopher Nelson, editor of Green Linden Press

"J.R. Solonche's poems are like translations from a language far more direct and intense than the English of everyday speech. And yet that speech is the very stuff his poems are made of. Solonche drills down to the core, the pith of the conversational moment."

— Hilary Sideris, author of *The Silent B* and *Un Amore Veloce*

Piano Music

J.R. Solonche

SERVING HOUSE BOOKS

Piano Music

Copyright © 2020 by J.R. Solonche

All Rights Reserved

Published by Serving House Books

Copenhagen, Denmark and South Orange, NJ

www.servinghousebooks.com

ISBN: 978-1-947175-33-4

Library of Congress Control Number: 2020942093

No part of this book may be used or reproduced in any manner whatsoever without the prior written permission of the copyright holder except for brief quotations in critical articles or reviews.

Member of The Independent Book Publishers Association

First Serving House Books Edition 2020

Cover Design: J.R. Solonche

Author Photograph: Emily Solonche

Serving House Books Logo: Barry Lereng Wilmont

BOOKS BY J.R. SOLONCHE

The Moon Is the Capital of the World
Enjoy Yourself
The Time of Your Life
For All I Know
The Porch Poems
To Say the Least
A Public Place
True Enough
If You Should See Me Walking on the Road
I, Emily Dickinson & Other Found Poems
The Jewish Dancing Master
Tomorrow, Today, and Yesterday
In Short Order
Heart's Content
Invisible
The Black Birch
Won't Be Long
Beautiful Day
Peach Girl: Poems for a Chinese Daughter (with Joan I. Siegel)

CONTENTS

Piano Music 11
The Ugliest Building 12
Near and Dear 13
It Was the Critic in Me 14
The Congolese Philosopher 15
Bourbon 16
Even You 17
So I Got Lost 18
There Is No Rule to the Exceptions 19
Greater Expectations 20
The Last Day of July at Last 21
The Bible in the Drawer in the Room in the Hotel 22
Now That 23
Conquest Conquers All 24
Apology 25
I Wanted to Tell the Woman 26
Disney 27
August 28
Paul the Bartender 29
Take Me Out to the Ball Game 30
Gravity 31
The Cloudburst 32
The Poets 33
Cinderellas 34
Morning Conversation 35
A Hawk in August 36
And Then in the Arms of the Galaxy with the Spiral Arms 37
And Thus We Shall Surrender 38
When We Think of Nothing 39
I'm Fine 40
When the Clock Broke 41
Augustulus 42
The Cloud 43
The Black Butterfly 44
A Pen Makes a Good Drum Stick 45
I Wore My Tee Shirt 46

It Is Not Meant to Be Beautiful 47
On My Seventy-Third Birthday 48
When One 49
My Neighbor 50
If Right Now 51
Cynicism 52
Neglect 52
One Thing after Another 54
Simultaneity 55
Trial and Error 56
There Are So Many Insects 57
The Single Propeller Plane 58
Chief Pontiac: A Syllabic Poem 59
The Bald Eagle 60
Island Eye Land Aye Land I Land 61
The Crickets 62
Orchards 63
For One Who Is So Cowardly 64
The Thunder Was in the East 65
A Case of Unmistakable Identity 66
Do You Miss the Good Old Days? 67
If You Cannot Be Yourself, Be a Mystery 68
Three Barns 69
Eighteen Nightmares 70
A Fairy Tale 72
Enough Is Enough 73
The More the This Then the Less the That 74
How Is It, But It Is, Possible 75
Not Good 76
Main Street 77
It's Too Bad 78
Very Short Ode to Corn 79
Very Short Ode to a Peach 80
Very Short Ode to a Dried Plum 81
Very Short Ode to My Notebook 82
Very Short Ode to My Pen 83
Very Short Ode to Ink 84
Very Short Ode to Money 85
Very Short Ode to an Umbrella 86
Very Short Ode to a Spider Web 87
Very Short Ode to an Acorn 88

Very Short Ode to a Marigold 89
Very Short Ode to a Wheelbarrow 90
Very Short Ode to a Vase 91
Very Short Ode to a Red-Headed Woodpecker 92
Very Short Ode to the Telephone 93
Much Is to Be Made from Little While Little Is to Be Made from Much 94
What's in a Name? 95
I Never Tire of the Clouds 96
Dark Photons 97
Apportionment 98
The Four Bikers of the Apocalypse 99

About the Author 101

PIANO MUSIC

The piano is tired of waiting.
The piano closes up shop.
The piano, a three-legged black stallion, wants to gallop away.
The piano's forte is silence.
The piano says, "Hands off."
The piano keeps its thoughts to itself.
The piano possesses the keys to the kingdom.
The piano knows black plus white does not equal gray.
The piano knows black plus white equals blue.
(Nota Bene: The piano knows its way.)
The piano says, "Follow me."
The piano says, "I'm in your hands."
The piano is depressed when it is not depressed.
The piano tunes out cacophony.
The piano spits out phony.
The piano doesn't stand on formality although formal.
The piano hugs its little sister harp.
The piano makes a grand entrance.
The piano always speaks true although not always uprightly.
The piano is touched by your sincerity.
The piano touches you with 88 fingers.
The piano touches you.

THE UGLIEST BUILDING

The ugliest building
in town is a church.
The prettiest building
in town is a church.
If I were a churchgoer,
I would go to the ugly
church on Sundays and
go to look at the pretty
church on all the others.
Hell, this I already do.

NEAR AND DEAR

Some things are near
but not dear.

Other things are dear
but not near.

Only two things are
both near and dear.

One is the one you most love.
The other is the one you most hate.

IT WAS THE CRITIC IN ME

It was the Critic in Me.
He was rattling his cage.
I unlocked it. I let him out.
"Go ahead," I said. "All's fair
in love, war, and poetry.
I'll stay out of your way,"
I said. "But only for a little while.
I can't have you running wild."
"I'll be quick," he said. "I won't
play him long. I'll make short
work of him." And so he did.
It was child's play.

THE CONGOLESE PHILOSOPHER

The Congolese philosopher
being interviewed on PBS
is a philosopher from the Congo,
and therefore just a tedious as
any other philosopher from
anywhere else, which is a shame
because I was hoping to hear some
real Congolese philosophy for a change.

BOURBON

It may not be
the be-all and end-all,
but it is the in-between-all.

EVEN YOU

Even you didn't know what to do.
Even you couldn't speak.
Even you slapped your forehead.
Even you sat back in your chair.
Even you couldn't come up with the words.
Even you to whom everyone looked.
Even you at whom everyone gestured with palms.
Even you who was farthest away.
Even you who was least sentimental.
Even you who was nearest the door.

SO I GOT LOST

So I went inside.
So I sat at the table by the window.

So I sat in the chair facing the door.
So the server came over to serve me.

So I said water.
So the server came with the water.

So I said the moon.
So the server said the full moon or the half moon.

So I said the full moon.
So the server said with the clouds or with the stars.

So I said with the stars.
So the server said with which wine.

So I said with which wine.
So the server said with the white.

So I said with the white.
So the server came with the full moon, the stars and the white wine.

So I had the full moon, the stars, and the white wine.
So I went outside.

So in the sky was no moon.
So in the sky were no stars.

So in the sky were only clouds.
So it was dark.

So I got lost.
So I went inside.

THERE IS NO RULE TO THE EXCEPTIONS

Anything went.
Anything goes.
Anything will go.

This took the whole class.
This takes the whole class.
This will take the whole class.

But they failed anyway.
But they fail anyway.
But they will fail anyway.

There were no rules.
There are no rules.
There will be no rules.

There always were a few exceptions.
There always are a few exceptions.
There always will be a few exceptions.

Thank goodness there were.
Thank goodness there are.
Thank goodness there will be.

GREATER EXPECTATIONS

What did you expect?
What did you expect from me?
What did you expect from him?
What did you expect from her?
What did you expect from them?
What did you expect from it?
What did you expect from us?
Did you expect me to be there?
Did you expect him to be taller?
Did you expect her to be slimmer?
Did you expect them to be more like you?
Did you expect it to be warmer?
Did you expect us to be more persuasive?
What did you expect?

THE LAST DAY OF JULY AT LAST

Someone must have sighed that.
Was it you?
Was it you who sighed the last day of July at last?
You must have been counting the days.
Or someone must sigh it yet.
Will it be you?
Will it be you who sighs the last day of July at last next July?
I could sigh it.
I could sigh the last of July at last on this last day of July.
And I have reason to.
There's money in the bank.
What will it be for, the money in the bank?
Will it be for spending on a big expense?
Will it be for just being money in the bank?
I like that.
I like money.
I like the look of money.
I like the look of money for being just money in the bank.
I like the look of money for being just money in the bank on the last day in July.

THE BIBLE IN THE DRAWER IN THE ROOM IN THE HOTEL

It was never opened.
I was the first to open it.
It felt good.
It felt bad.
I did not open it to read it.
I read it once.
I will never read it again.
I opened it to hear it crack.
The same as the new textbooks in school.
I liked to hear them crack.
It cracked the crack of the shell of a nut.
It cracked the crack of a cockroach stepped upon.
It cracked the crack of an ice cube in a glass of whiskey.
It cracked the crack of a wishbone.
It felt good.
It felt bad.

NOW THAT

Now that that
ash tree is cut
down and out
of the way,
the new light
can light the way
for new trees to
come in that way.

CONQUEST CONQUERS ALL

There is only one Mt. Everest.
But that doesn't stop them.
There is also, and there is also, and there is also.

There is only one Mt. Everest.
So that is the only prize worth prizing.
So that is the only dying worth dying.

There is only one Mt. Everest.
Of Mt. Everest there is only one.
There is only one, there is only one, there is only one.

APOLOGY

Brother Hummingbird,
I am sorry. I apologize
to you for not filling
your feeder with the sugar
water that you are looking
for. I will make it up to you,
Brother Hummingbird,
tomorrow with the most
costly pure cane sugar
and the most expensive
water bottled at the deepest,
most inaccessible spring
of all the springs in the world.

I WANTED TO TELL THE WOMAN

I wanted to tell the woman
with the umbrella the same
cloudless sky blue as the cloudless
blue of the sky on a day cloudless
blue how foolish she looked on
the street among all those black
umbrellas, but there I was in
the rain with no umbrella at all.

DISNEY

He hated Jews.
I hated Mickey Mouse.
We were even.

AUGUST

What is August meant to
mean to the petunias except
more of the same sun as July,
more of the same rain? What
is August meant to mean to
the oaks except more of
the same sun as July, more
of the same rain?

PAUL THE BARTENDER

Paul the bartender was wearing
a tee shirt picturing a nun
smoking a cigarette. It read,
"Holy smokes!" "Paul," I said.
"Great tee shirt, but a better one
would be a nun on a toilet
with the words, "Holy shit!"
"You're right," he said. "But
I couldn't find that one, and
anyway the boss wouldn't
approve." "But you're the boss,"
I said. "I mean my wife. She
doesn't smoke, but she does shit."

TAKE ME OUT TO THE BALLGAME

Take me out to the ballgame.
Take me out to the crowd.
Buy me some peanuts and crackerjacks.
I don't care if I never get back.

Take me out to the ballgame.
There is wisdom in the crowd.
The crowd knows how to cheer.
The crowd knows how to boo.

Take me out to the ballgame.
Buy me some peanuts in moderation.
The salt is good on a hot day.
The salt replaces your electrolytes.

Take me out to the ballgame.
I never liked crackerjacks.
I opened the box from the bottom to get the prize.
I gave the crackerjacks to the pigeons.

Take me out to the ballgame.
Take me out. Take me out.
I don't care if I never get back.
I don't care. I don't care.

GRAVITY

They say no one
knows what it is,
not even the physicists
who are the ones
who ought to know.
Not Newton, not
Einstein, not Hawking.
But I know. I know
what gravity is, and
I will take the secret
to my grave.

THE CLOUDBURST

The cloudburst
was brief but broke
heat's choke hold long
enough to let
the cooler air exhale.

THE POETS

"Who are your favorite poets?" someone asked.
"Dickinson, Whitman, Williams, and the namer of the beers
at the Long Lot Farm Brewery on Johnson Road
in Blooming Grove, New York," I answered.

CINDERELLAS

There's the Cinderella who has red hair.
There's the Cinderella who speaks Chinese.
There's the Cinderella who has brothers.
There's the Cinderella who's obese.
There's the Cinderella who's bulimic.
There's the Cinderella who's adopted.
There's the Cinderella who's a runaway.
There's the Cinderella who writes bad poetry.
There's the Cinderella who writes good poetry.
There's the Cinderella who builds model planes.
There's the Cinderella who's paraplegic.
There's the Cinderella who's gay.
There's the Cinderella who has insomnia.
There's the Cinderella who makes the best frog's legs in the kingdom.
There's the Cinderella who turns into a frog.
There's the Catholic Cinderella who converts to marry a Jewish prince.

MORNING CONVERSATION

"Good morning, Hydrangea," I said
"Good morning," said the hydrangea.
"How are you?" I said.
"Oh, I'm all right," it said.
"You sure?" I said
"You don't mind spending your whole life behind the deer fence?"
"Not at all," it said.
"Considering the alternative."
"Of course," I said.
"I, too, have had to consider alternatives.
And many more than you."
"Maybe," it said.
"But they all come down to just one, don't they?" it said.
 "Good morning, Petunias," I said.

A HAWK IN AUGUST

The wings span the better part of an eagle.
The wings span the best part of the afternoon.
The wings span the best part of an emperor.
The wings span the better part of an empire.
The wings span the best part of the American part.

AND THEN IN THE ARMS OF THE GALAXY WITH THE SPIRAL ARMS

And then I shall spiral out of control.
And then I shall sing the sad cradle song.

And then I shall spiral out of control.
And then I shall sing the sad lullaby.

And then I shall spiral out of control.
And then I shall sing the sad love song.

And then I shall spiral out of control.
And then I shall sing the sad funeral dirge.

And then I shall spiral out of control.
And then I shall spiral in the arms of the galaxy with the spiral arms.

AND THUS WE SHALL SURRENDER

And thus we shall surrender to the first wind that blows.
And thus we shall surrender to the first ship that spies us.
And thus we shall surrender to the first horseman that passes by.
And thus how sweet it will be to surrender.
And thus how liberating it will be to give up.
And thus we shall be as we were before all that standing up.
And thus we shall be as we were before all that holding on.
And thus we shall be as we were before all that obstinacy.
And thus we shall be as we were before all that.

WHEN WE THINK OF NOTHING

When we think of nothing,
which means when we do not think
of anything at all, which means
when we are not thinking,
we are thinking of the soul.

I'M FINE

I'm fine
with criticism
as long as
the criticism
is finely
tuned, pitched
perfectly to
the critical ear.
In other words,
make me a believer.

WHEN THE CLOCK BROKE

When the clock broke, time died.
So I brought time to the time repair shop.
The time repairman examined Time.
"I can repair your time," he said.
"How much will it cost?" I said.
He told me how much.
"How much is a new time?" I said.
He told me how much.
"I can repair this time," he said.
"It will be as good as new."
"Okay," I said. "Go ahead and fix
my old time if it will be as good as new."
"But it only comes with a one-year warranty," he said.
"But you said it will be as good as new," I said.
"That's right," he said.
 "That's what we time repairmen call a paradox."

AUGUSTULUS

Someone had to be last.
Someone had to close the door behind him.
Someone had to break the last sword in half.
Someone had to burn everything.
Someone had to ride the last horse away.
Someone had to take the fall for the fall.

THE CLOUD

The cloud this afternoon idles
in the sky so beautifully
even its shadow is as handsome
as a matinee idol.

THE BLACK BUTTERFLY

The black butterfly
right side up
on the ground
looks like an upside
down baby bat upside up.

A PEN MAKES A GOOD DRUMSTICK

A pen makes a good drumstick.
You can drum the bourbon glass with it.
You can drum the tin table shaped like a flower with it.
You can drum the telephone with it.
You can drum away the seconds with it.
You can drum away the minutes with it.
You can try to drum away the hours with it, but you will fail.
You can drum away the poem with it.
You can drum away your pulse with it.
You can drum away your own sweet time with it.
You can beat the drum to beat the drum with it.
You can beat the devil with it.

I WORE MY TEE SHIRT

I wore my tee shirt
with the picture of a goat.
I wore it in case Jesus
comes back today to separate
the sheep and the goats in
the Last Judgment. I don't
need him to interview me,
ask me stupid questions about
my habits and predilections.
All he'll have to do is look
at my tee shirt, and he'll
know right away what
I am and that I want
to spend eternity in Hell
with all the other old goats.

IT IS NOT MEANT TO BE BEAUTIFUL

It is not meant to be beautiful,
the sky, the clouds in the sky,
the sun shining on the clouds
in the sky, even the jet between
the clouds in the sky with the sun
on its wings and fuselage.
It's not meant to be beautiful, so
why is it beautiful? And why
does it make me want to cry?

ON MY SEVENTY-THIRD BIRTHDAY

My candle is
extinguished
at both ends.

WHEN ONE

When one
of the owl pair
calls and there
is no answer,
I say a prayer.
And when,
from across
the road,
the call comes
of the other,
I say another
prayer, but one
too low to hear.

MY NEIGHBOR

My neighbor
is using
a circular saw
to saw circles
around my
afternoon.

IF RIGHT NOW

If right now
left now,
right now
would still
be left
right now.

CYNICISM

The two hummingbirds
are either lovers
or enemies. Oh, what
the hell. What I don't
know won't hurt me.

NEGLECT

The neglected pool behind
the neglected fence beside
the neglected house is full
of what the trees, of what
the geese, of what the raccoons,
of what the ground hogs, of what
the weeds have not neglected.

ONE THING AFTER ANOTHER

It isn't fair.
Why isn't it ever
another's turn
to be after one?

SIMULTANEITY

How else?
There is no other way.
It must all happen at once.
All, all must happen all at once.
All, all must happen at the same time.
It must all be simultaneous.
Or there will be nothing.
There will be nothing at all.
There will be nothing all at once.

TRIAL AND ERROR

The monarch butterfly
tried leaf after leaf after leaf after
leaf until it settled to settle on
the first leaf it tried.

THERE ARE SO MANY INSECTS

There are so many insects
sounding like insects
I don't know what insects
I'm listening to, and something
tells me it would make no
difference if I did.

THE SINGLE PROPELLER PLANE

The single propeller plane,
unseen, low enough
to be unseen behind trees
high enough to cover
its crossing, passes
through with the sound
of a drill drilling
through the solid green afternoon.

CHIEF PONTIAC: A SYLLABIC POEM

When I was a kid, I liked to look
at hood ornaments. They were the best
part of the cars. My favorite was Chief
Pontiac. It was made of Lucite.
It was translucent amber. His face,
sharp as a hawk's, cut through the air like
an arrow. He was the real thing. He
was a genuine red skin. I liked
that. I liked Indians who were real.
I liked Jay Silverheels, Tonto in
the movies. I liked that he was real.
I figured there weren't enough real
Indian actors in the movies
to play Indians, so the movies
had to hire whites to portray them.
Most of all, I liked to say the name
out loud. I liked to say, *Pontiac,*
Pontiac. Pontiac. Pontiac.
I would always know that the car that
was coming toward me on the road was
a Pontiac when I saw the sun's
gleam on the translucent amber head
of Chief Pontiac. It was the first
word my mouth played with. *PON—ti—ac. Pont—*
EE --ac. Pon – ti – AC was my first poem.

THE BALD EAGLE

"Hey, Emily," I said to my daughter.
I was outside. "I just saw the bald eagle."
She was in the kitchen. The window
was open. "It just flew right over my head.
The bald eagle," I said. She didn't hear me.
She was cooking. She was listening
to the radio. "Hey, I just saw the bald
eagle," I said to the hummingbird.
"It flew right over my head." It didn't
hear me. It was busy feeding at the feeder.
"Hey, I just saw the bald eagle," I said
to the crickets. "It flew right over my head."
They didn't hear me. They were making
too much noise among themselves.
"Hey, I just saw the bald eagle," I said
to the bee in the petunia. "It flew right
over my head." It didn't hear me.
It was preoccupied with its own thoughts.
"Hey, I just saw you," I said to the bald
eagle. "You flew right over my head."
"I hear you," the bald eagle said. "But
you're beneath my disdain."

ISLAND EYE LAND AYE LAND I LAND

Did you ever wish to be a sailor?
Did you ever wish to be a drunken sailor?
Did you ever wish to spend like a drunken sailor?
Did you ever wish to swear like a drunken sailor?
Did you ever wish to wear a sailor suit?
Did you ever wish to sail a toy sail boat in Central Park?
Did you ever wish to sail a sail boat in Long Island Sound?
Did you ever wish to sound like a captain of a sail boat?
Did you ever wish to give orders to subordinates?
Did you ever wish to be the captain of a submarine?
Did you ever wish to own your own island?
Did you ever wish to go down with the ship?

THE CRICKETS

The crickets
in the grass
made such a racket
I swear they said,
"Stay out of this.
Mind your own business."

ORCHARDS

"Wow, what big peaches," I said.
"Are they bigger than last year?"
"They are," the owner said. "But
there are fewer than last year."
"How come?" I said. "The weather,"
she said. "A lot of rain. More than
normal. And not enough sunny days
to dry things out a little. Less than
normal sun." "So it's a metaphor,"
I said. "How's that?" she said. "You
know," I said. "A short but gloriously
full life or a long but average life."
"I'd rather have a bigger harvest of
smaller peaches," she said. "My living
depends on it." " I'm the opposite,"
I said. "I'd rather have a handful
of glorious poems than a truckload
of average ones. My immortality
depends on it." "That's the difference
between poems and peaches, I suppose,"
she said. "By the way, I enjoyed your
new book. The peaches are free."

FOR ONE WHO IS SO COWARDLY

For one who is so cowardly,
how little you settle for to settle down.

For one who is so cowardly,
how shallow the shelter of your sleep.

For one who is so cowardly,
how long you bear the age of agony.

For one who is so cowardly,
how straight you stand against the wall.

For one who is so cowardly,
how smilingly you stare ahead unblinkingly.

For one who is so cowardly,
how short you are with the ignorant.

THE THUNDER WAS IN THE EAST

The thunder was in the east.
The passenger jet was in the west.
They shared the north and the south.
They were brothers.
One was right-handed.
One was left-handed.
One had a baritone voice.
One had a tenor voice.
Neither was louder than the other.
They were equally insistent for my attention.
Then they left and left the sky alone.

A CASE OF UNMISTAKABLE IDENTITY

Have you ever been mistaken for someone else?
Have you ever been mistaken for the one with the convertible?
Have you ever been mistaken for the one with the beautiful wife?
Have you ever been mistaken for the one with the seven hunting dogs?
Have you ever been mistaken for the doctor?
Have you ever been mistaken for the pharmacist?
Have you ever been mistaken for the real estate agent?
Have you ever been mistaken for the high school gym teacher?
Have you ever been mistaken for the middle school Spanish teacher?
Have you ever been mistaken for the elementary school music teacher?
Have you ever been mistaken for you know, that actor, what's his name?
Have you ever been mistaken for you know, that singer, what's his name?
Have you ever been mistaken for you know, that stand-up comic, what's his name?
Have you ever been mistaken for you?

DO YOU EVER MISS THE GOOD OLD DAYS?

Do you ever miss the old sod?
Do you ever miss that old time religion?
Do you ever miss those golden oldies?
Do you ever miss that old gang of yours?
Do you ever miss the old gray mare?
Do you ever miss the old school tie?
Do you ever miss that old man river?
Do you ever miss old man winter?
Do you ever miss your old man?
Do you ever miss your old lady?
Do you ever miss the same old thing?
Do you ever miss any old place?
Do you ever miss your old Kentucky home?
Do you ever miss the old woman who lived in a shoe?
Do you ever miss any old thing?

IF YOU CANNOT BE YOURSELF, BE A MYSTERY

Or if you can be yourself, be a mystery.
Or if you don't want to be yourself, be a mystery.
Or if you are still finding yourself, be a mystery.
Or if you've already found yourself, be a mystery.
Or if you want to lose yourself, be a mystery.
Or if you already are a mystery to others, be a mystery to yourself.
Or if you cannot be a mystery to yourself, be a mystery to others.
Or if you cannot be a mystery, be mysterious.

THREE BARNS

Even in collapse,
they are different in decay.
Each has its own way
of going down,
of giving ground to ground.
This one's roof is gone.
That one's covered but falls
into the space of the missing wall.
And that one is all roof.
That's all.

EIGHTEEN NIGHTMARES

I am in a snare.
Ants are eating me.
Satan stares.

I am in a snare.
Rats are eating me.
Satan grins.

I am in a snare.
Sin is in the air.
Satan sings.

I am in a thin shirt.
A giant is eating
my heart.

Mars rises in the east.
I rise to meet it.
It's a near miss.

I'm hanging in an ash tree.
Satan is sneering
at me.

She hits me,
She hits me, hits me, hits me.
She's a hammer.

Again it's math time.
Again I'm the tangent.
Again I'm the target

I smite the giant.
She's mine.
She marries me.

It's the rite site.
I'm at the rear.
I might mate right there.

I'm against a gate
in a street that isn't straight.
Satan greets me.

It is raining.
I'm in the game.
There's a smear, a rip, a tear.

Theresa has great tits.
I eat them.
I taste grease.

I am a great singer.
I miss the high A.
I hear, *Hiss, hiss, hiss.*

I am high.
She is smarter.
She is higher than I.

It is night.
I am in a harness.
A giant gnat is harassing me.

I am Mars.
She is Hera.
I am not right; neither is she.

Her name is Serena.
I ram her.
Her hair is tar.

A FAIRY TALE

Once upon a time, Once-Upon-A-Time wanted to be an ending and not a beginning. It was tired of being a beginning all the time. It envied Happily-Ever-After who was never tired of being the happy ending all the time. So Once-Upon-A-Time went to the palace to see The-King. "What do you want?" asked The-King. "I am tired of being the beginning all the time," said Once-Upon-A-Time. "I want to be the happy ending like Happily-Ever-After." "Makes no difference to me who the beginning is or who the ending is," said The-King. "Just as long as I'm in the middle of it all and my daughter The-Princess is happy." "So I can be the ending?" said Once-Upon-A-Time. "Sure, why not?" said The-King. "But what would you have me do with Happily-Ever-After?" "Well, he can take my place at the beginning," said Once-Upon-A-Time. "I see," said The-King. "Okay, let's give it a try." The-King sent for Happily-Ever-After. "Listen," said The-King. "I have decided that you, Happily-Ever-After, trade places with Once-Upon-A-Time. Understood?" "Well, no," said Happily-Ever-After. "I don't understand, but you're The-King, so I'll give it a try." And give it a try they did. One try after another. One fairy tale after another. But try as they might, it just didn't work. Everybody was confused and laughed at them and blamed The-King and The-Princess was not happy. Moral of the story: Never make The-Princess cry. Second Moral of the story: Never blame The-King.

ENOUGH IS ENOUGH

There's a wasp
at the hummingbird
feeder. Every time
the hummingbird
approaches, the wasp
chases it off. Fuck
this! I'm going to kill
that son-of-a-bitch.

THE MORE THE THIS THEN THE LESS THE THAT

Equations are for
the fastidious,
for the obsessive-
compulsive, for
the algebrists
among us, for
the fools of balance,
for the children
of see-saw sense.
An old man knows
the difference
between one thing
and another, between
doing and done,
between going and gone,
between the earth
and the world.

HOW IS IT, BUT IT IS, POSSIBLE

How is it, but it is, possible
to love loneliness, for
I have done it, loved loneliness,
and you, too, I am sure of it, yes,
that you, too, have loved loneliness
and still do probably, or why
are you reading this if not because
you either love poetry or love loneliness?

NOT GOOD

If you said you would,
but you won't,
that's not good.

If you said you could,
but you can't,
that's not good.

If you said you should,
but you don't,
that's not good.

If you said you've understood,
but you haven't,
that's not good.

If you said you're good,
but you're not,
that's not good.

MAIN STREET

It's where you go to look in windows.
It's where you go to read the news.
It's where you go to see the widows.
It's where you go to hear the blues.

It's where to go to buy the duct tape.
It's where to go to drink the beer.
It's where to go to eat a crepe.
It's where you go to sniff and sneer.

It's where you go to get the coffees.
It's where you go to get a snip.
It's where you go to see divorcees.
It's where you go to get a grip.

It's there, there, all there is is there.
It's where you go to be somewhere.

IT'S TOO BAD

It's too bad I never served.
It's too bad my eyes were so bad.
It's too bad my eyes kept me out.
It's too bad I couldn't see the top line on the chart.
It's too bad I couldn't see the chart on the wall.
It's too bad I couldn't see the wall.
It's too bad they zee'd me out.
It's too bad they didn't want me.
It's too bad because they would have put me in intelligence.
It's too bad I didn't have a chance to give them the wrong intelligence.
It's too bad I didn't save the life of one child by giving them the wrong intelligence.
It's too bad I wasn't given a dishonorable discharge.
It's too bad I couldn't frame it.
It's too bad I couldn't hang it on the wall.
It's too damn bad I never served in fucking Vietnam.

VERY SHORT ODE TO CORN

Sun on
a stalk!

You look
like father
but sustain
like mother!

The god in
the goddess
is as god
in goddess.

Sun on
a stalk!

VERY SHORT ODE TO A PEACH

Whenever I see
a peach,

I want
to reach

out for it
and beseech

the peach,
"O, Peach!"

VERY SHORT ODE TO A DRIED PLUM

How old you look,
dried plum, so old
you look like a prune,
so wrinkled and leathery,
so shriveled and sun burned,
that every day I desire
you, I desire four of you,
to keep me regular so
that I will never look
as old as you, never
ever as old as you,
Dried Plum!

VERY SHORT ODE TO MY NOTEBOOK

O, open-minded one!
O, beautiful blue-veined butterfly!

I thank you.
I thank you for being here.

I thank you for opening yourself up to me.
I thank you for letting me fill your space with my inscrutability.

I thank you for your blank stare.
I thank you for your silent dare.

VERY SHORT ODE TO MY PEN

O, ink-arrow, O, where
would you be now
if not now in my hand?
Would you be now
writing a shopping list?
Would you be now
signing a check?
Would you be now
penning a letter
to a distant cousin?
Or would you be now
writing a poem better than
"Very Short Ode to My Pen"?

VERY SHORT ODE TO INK

O, ink!
You are the blood of poetry!
You are the tears of the poets!
You are the blue of the sea!
You are the bottomless blue of the sea!
O, ink, I do not know where you have come from,
but you are welcome to stay here forever!
O, ink!

VERY SHORT ODE TO MONEY

O, money!
Where the hell did you come from?
What sort of word are you, anyway?
Money, are you from the Roman goddess *Juno Moneta?*
Money, money, money.
You are funny, funny, funny.
You two rhyme so well.
You must be twins.
Funny money, funny money, funny money.
They say you cannot buy me happiness.
I say, That's funny.
I say, So what?
I say you can buy me everything else.
I say you can buy me immortality.
What else are you good for?
O, money!

VERY SHORT ODE TO AN UMBRELLA

O, umbrella!
O, beautiful invention of inversion!
O, portable collapsible roof over my head!
I pray for rain, so I can carry you out into the world.
I pray for rain, so I can offer your shelter to the lovely lady
on the street who has neglected to bring hers.
I pray for rain, O, umbrella!
O, umbrella big enough for two!

VERY SHORT ODE TO A SPIDER WEB

O, spider web!
O, web of science!
What an engineering feat you are!
How fine and delicate yet how strong!
How precise and defined!
How perfect in measurement!
How mathematically exact!
Where is the genius who made you?
Ah, there she is.
There she is in the dark corner of her creation.
I would ask her to come forward for a bow.
But I shall not, for she is hungry.
O, web of desire!
O, web of art!

VERY SHORT ODE TO AN ACORN

O, seed of the mighty oak!
So many thousands upon thousands of you
did my ancestors gather in the forests of Poland.
And now I their descendent gather only you.
How far have I carried your name from the forests of Poland.
O, seed of the mighty oak!

VERY SHORT ODE TO A MARIGOLD

O, golden-yellow marigold!
How wonderfully you are hold-
ing your own under all the rain!
How bravely you are hold-
out for the sun!
O, golden-yellow marigold!

VERY SHORT ODE TO A WHEELBARROW

O, plain prosaic wheelbarrow!
I sense your sorrow.
You are not red.
You are not glazed with rain water.
You are not beside the white chickens.
Yet so much depends upon you.
Yet you are beloved.
O, plain prosaic wheelbarrow!

VERY SHORT ODE TO A VASE

O, shapely porcelain vase!
I will not call you vase.
I will call you hollow sculpture.
For that is what you are.
No flowers for you, O hollow sculpture!
No flowers for you, for I will not call you vase.
Not ever a flower for you no matter how much you beg.
O, white and shapely porcelain hollow sculpture!

VERY SHORT ODE TO A RED-HEADED WOODPECKER

Red-headed woodpecker!
What shall I call you?
Shall I call you cobbler bird?
Shall I call you carpenter bird?
Shall I call you Jesus bird?
Yes, I shall call you Jesus bird
for you are brethren in carpentry.
Jesus bird, I hear your sermon on the tree.
And I believe it, every word!

VERY SHORT ODE TO THE TELEPHONE

O, telephone!
O, mechanism of the mouth of miles and miles!
You are my best companion!
You are my worst enemy!
Only you know but will not say.
I hear your ringing in my ears.
I hear your singing of the saddest song.
O, telephone!

MUCH IS TO BE MADE FROM LITTLE WHILE LITTLE IS TO BE MADE FROM MUCH

For example, the crickets tell the grass what to say.
For example, one small cloud the shape of an ear listens in.
For example, the hornet knows better than the ants and does not drown in the hummingbird feeder.
For example, the dragonfly lives no longer than it has to.
For example, the sharp-shinned hawk doesn't care about your whereabouts.
For example, when the coyotes howl from the other side of the lake, I stop what I'm doing.
For example, one small breeze is enough to lift all the elm's leaves.
For example, when the owl falls silent, I listen more carefully.
For example, the rain is reticent and asks my permission.
For example, from time to time the moon needs its privacy so disappears.
For example, the rain clouds pass without rain.
For example, the train's the soloist tonight.
For example, my neighbor's motorcycle sounds sick.
For example, the woodpecker dreams he is a hummingbird.
For example, the stream dreams it is a river.
For example, the river dreams it is the ocean.
For example, the ocean dreams it is the world.

WHAT'S IN A NAME

I went to Glenmere
Brewery. I had a *Lucid
Dragon*. If I made beer,
I'd call it *Lucid Poet*.
How's that for a rare brew?

I NEVER TIRE OF THE CLOUDS

I never tire of the clouds.
I never tire of their shapes.
I never tire of their whites and grays.
I never tire of their shadows on the ground through which I walk
as if through a valley in the sky.

DARK PHOTONS

Dark photons
explain all.
That's what
he said. He's
a physicist.
He says things
like that. Dark
photons explain
all. I could say
things like that.
I could say dark
photons explain
all. But I'm a poet
so I won't.

APPORTIONMENT

After the rain, each one finds
its manna in the manner of its size,
as now the paper wasp sips a lifetime
from a drop to wander once more
the desert of the air.

THE FOUR BIKERS OF THE APOCALYPSE

They passed slowly, as slowly
as they could while still able
to pass me. And they made noise,
as much noise as they could while
still able to go so slowly. And
I have to say, they did unnerve me.
I have to say, the first thing I thought
of was the *Apocalypse* and its Four
Horsemen. Death. Famine. Pestilence.
War. I have to say, it fit them perfectly.

ABOUT THE AUTHOR

 J.R. Solonche is the author of nineteen books of poetry and coauthor of another. He lives in the Hudson Valley.

www.ingramcontent.com/pod-product-compliance
Lightning Source LLC
Chambersburg PA
CBHW022013120526
44592CB00034B/806